PICTURE LIBRARY

SPIDERS

PICTURE LIBRARY

SPIDERS

Norman Barrett

Franklin Watts

London   New York   Sydney   Toronto

© 1989 Franklin Watts Ltd

First published in Great Britain
    1989 by
Franklin Watts Ltd
12a Golden Square
London W1R 4BA

First published in the USA by
Franklin Watts Inc
387 Park Avenue South
New York
NY 10016

First published in Australia by
Franklin Watts
14 Mars Road
Lane Cove
NSW 2066

UK ISBN: 0 86313 813 6
US ISBN: 0–531–10702–7
Library of Congress Catalog Card
Number 88–51514

Printed in Italy

Designed by
Barrett & Weintroub

Photographs by
Survival Anglia
Michael Chinery
Pat Morris
Mansell Collection
NASA

Illustration by
Rhoda & Robert Burns

Technical Consultant
Michael Chinery

Contents

Introduction

Spiders are eight-legged creatures of all shapes and sizes. The smallest is about the size of the period at the end of this sentence. The largest, one of the bird-eating spiders, has a leg spread that would cover this page from top to bottom.

All spiders spin silk. Some spin webs to catch their prey. Other spiders run after their prey or lie in wait for it.

△ A spider with a fly caught in its web, wrapped in silk and ready to eat. Many spiders spin webs to catch insects that fly into the fine, sticky threads.

Spiders live in all parts of the world, wherever they can get food. They are found in gardens, fields, houses, woods, deserts and even in water. They live on insects and other small animals.

All spiders have fangs. They inject poison into their prey to kill it. But few spiders are harmful to people.

△ A desert tarantula, one of the world's largest spiders. Tarantula is the common name for all kinds of very large, hairy spiders.

7

Looking at spiders

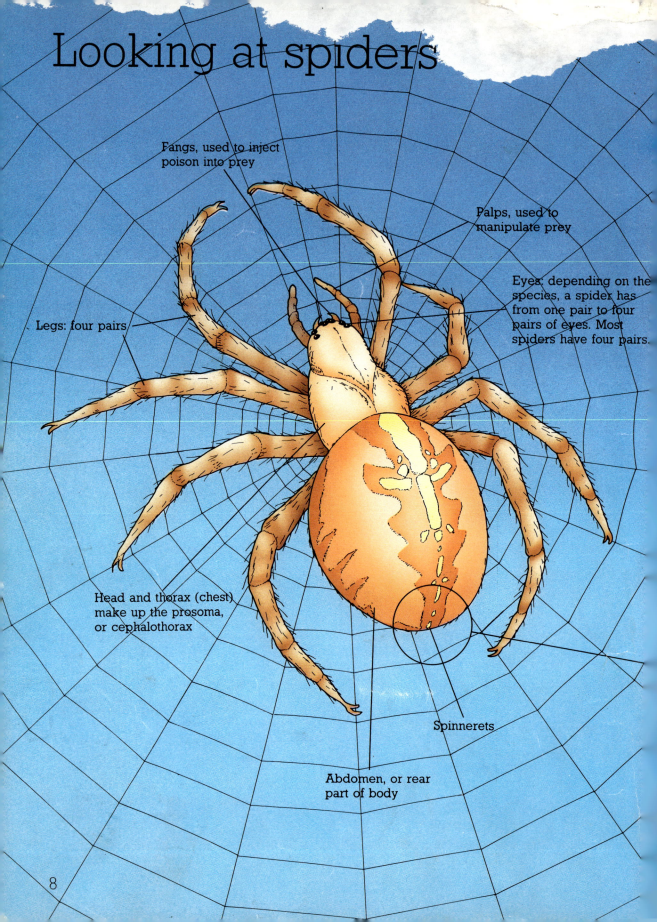

Fangs, used to inject poison into prey

Palps, used to manipulate prey

Eyes: depending on the species, a spider has from one pair to four pairs of eyes. Most spiders have four pairs.

Legs: four pairs

Head and thorax (chest) make up the prosoma, or cephalothorax

Spinnerets

Abdomen, or rear part of body

Making

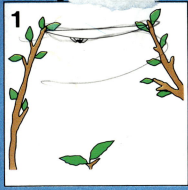  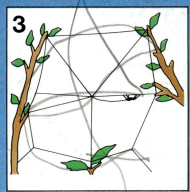

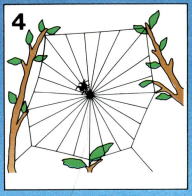 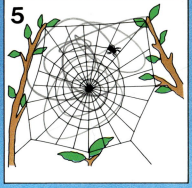 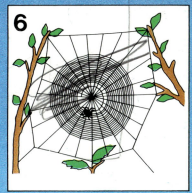

1 Bridging the gap.
2 Fixing the first spokes.
3 Completing the framework.

4 Completing the spokes.
5 Spinning out a dry spiral.
6 Completing the sticky spiral.

Spinnerets

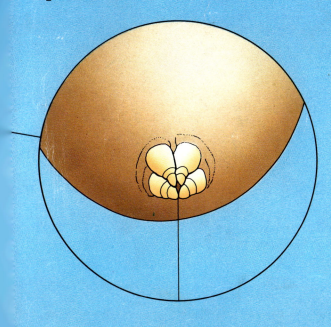

The spinnerets are the silk-spinning organs. Most kinds of spiders have six spinnerets. Liquid silk flows from silk glands in the spider's abdomen through the spinnerets to the outside. The spider presses its spinnerets against something to attach the silk, and then moves away to draw it out. The liquid silk hardens as it is being stretched.

Spiders have various types of silk glands that produce silk for different purposes. The framework of the web above, for example, is spun with dry silk. The spider then works from the dry spiral to spin a sticky spiral.

Making and using silk

Spiders spin various kinds of silk used for special purposes. They make thin or thick thread, dry or sticky thread. Silk is used for making webs and nests, for lining burrows and for wrapping up prey. Female spiders enclose their eggs in an egg sac, a bag made of silk.

A spider always spins a silk thread, called a dragline, behind itself as it moves about. If threatened, it can drop to safety from its dragline.

▷ A spider cocoon hangs from a silken thread. Most types of spiders enclose their eggs in an egg sac. They then wrap the sac in a special kind of silk, often to make it strong and waterproof. They might hang this cocoon from their web or from a twig or small branch.

▽ A spider's silk is extremely strong. Even a large spider such as this one can be supported on a fine thread.

Birth of spiders

Some kinds of spiders stay with the egg sac until the baby spiders, or spiderlings, hatch. Others carry the sac with them wherever they go.

An average size spider lays about 100 eggs. Spiderlings hatch inside the egg sac and stay there until warm weather arrives. They tear a tiny hole in the sac, and once they are out start spinning draglines.

△ A female wolf spider carries her egg sac wherever she goes until the eggs are ready to hatch. She then attaches the egg sac to a plant and covers it with a silken tent. Some other types of spiders also carry their egg sacs.

▷ A mass of spiderlings ride on the back of their mother. The wolf spider carries her young in this way until their second molt (shedding of the skin), when they are able to go off by themselves.

▽ A nursery web spider makes a nursery for her spiderlings. Just before the eggs are due to hatch, she attaches her egg sac to a leaf or other suitable structure and weaves a kind of tent over it to protect the newly born spiderlings.

Web spinners

Spiders spin many different kinds of webs. The most beautifully made are those of the orb weavers. These have "spokes" of dry silk connected by spiral threads of sticky silk for trapping insects.

Some orb weavers spin a new web every night. Others repair their webs if they are damaged.

Sheet-web weavers make a sheet of tangled threads attached to a support. Cobwebs in the home are dust-laden sheet webs.

▽ An orb weaver lies in wait for its prey. Some orb weavers stay in the center of their webs. Others attach a line to the center of the web, holding it as they hide nearby. When an insect gets trapped in the web, the line vibrates.

Some orb weavers spin zigzag bands of shiny white silk called stabilimenta in their webs. It is thought that this is to probably camouflage the spider and make the spiders invisible on the web.

Hammock weavers spin flat or slightly domed sheets in grass, bushes and other vegetation. They spin a tangle of threads above the silken sheet to knock flying insects into it.

△ The orb web of a garden spider outlined in morning dew. It takes the spider about an hour to weave such an intricate web.

△ Hammock webs trap flying insects that fall into them. The spider usually hangs upside down under the web, ready to spear her prey with her fangs from below.

▷ A fishing-net spider hangs suspended by its back feet while it holds its net out over a leaf. It will drop its net over an insect to trap it, and then eat net and insect together.

◁ The common house spider, which makes tangled sheet webs.

△ A communal spiders' web, used by many spiders. Most spiders are solitary animals, living alone. But some kinds, mostly in hot lands, share the same network of webs. They each spin their own webs, but the result is an irregular mesh.

◁ Daddy longlegs spiders may be so called because they look like the long-legged insects called craneflies, although of course they have no wings. They build flimsy webs and use their long legs to throw more silk over trapped flies.

Some web spinning spiders are dangerous to human beings. Perhaps the best known of these is the black widow.

Black widows spin untidy webs in dark corners. Their bite can cause severe illness and pain if not treated with an antitoxin (cure).

They usually retreat to their webs when frightened. They bite only if a person or animal accidentally comes into contact with them.

▽ The black widow spider, one of the few web spinners dangerous to humans. It gets its name because the female sometimes kills the male after mating, although it is not the only kind of spider to do so.

Tarantulas

Tarantulas have large, hairy bodies and long legs, but most of them are harmless to people. They live in warm climates.

Many kinds of tarantulas dig burrows and make nests in them. These include trap-door spiders and bird-eating spiders. Tarantulas do not build webs.

The name tarantula was originally given to some of the larger wolf spiders, but is now commonly used for any large, hairy spider.

▷ The orange-kneed tarantula is often kept as a pet. Tarantulas must be handled carefully. They can deliver a painful bite and their hairs can irritate people's skin. They could be seriously hurt or even killed if dropped.

▽ A bird-eating spider of New Guinea. There are several kinds of bird-eating spiders. They live in trees in the tropics. They do eat small birds, but live mainly on lizards, frogs and small snakes.

△ A white lady spider digs a tunnel in an African desert (left). It hides inside its tunnel, coming out only to capture prey, such as a cricket (above). Many kinds of trap-door spider spin a silken door over the entrance to their burrows and leap out only for a split second to grab a passing insect.

◁ A baboon spider, a large African tarantula.

Hunting spiders

Spiders that do not make webs to catch their prey are called hunting spiders. They include wolf spiders, jumping spiders and crab spiders.

Wolf spiders, with good eyesight and long legs, are excellent hunters. Most kinds do not have settled homes. They catch their prey by chasing it.

Jumping spiders creep up on their prey and pounce on it. Crab spiders hide from their prey and suddenly grab the unsuspecting victims.

▽ A wolf spider on a leaf. Wolf spiders are common in woods and fields. They usually chase their prey on the ground, although they do not run very far.

◁ A jumping spider from Indonesia. Jumping spiders have large eyes and excellent eyesight. They stalk their prey like a cat, before pouncing and biting it with their poisonous fangs. Most kinds of jumping spiders are small, measuring less than 5 mm (0.2 in).

▽ Jumping spiders of the tropics are among the most colorful of all spiders.

△ A yellow crab spider, camouflaged on a flower, catches an unsuspecting fly. Some crab spiders can change their color to match different blossoms.

▷ Crab spiders have short, wide bodies and look like crabs. They can walk backward and sideways like crabs, too.

Other hunting spiders include the ground hunting spiders. They live under rocks and stones and come out at night to hunt for prey, which they recognize by touch.

Woodlouse killers are ground hunting spiders found in many parts of the world. They are slow-moving, but fast enough to catch the woodlice that share their habitat. Unlike most other spiders, they seem to find woodlice tasty.

△ The woodlouse killer has large, powerful fangs that enable it to pierce the body armor of the woodlouse.

Raft spiders

Raft spiders are hunting spiders that live on or near water, usually in swampy areas. They prey upon insects, tadpoles and tiny fish.

   Most raft spiders spend their time sitting on floating leaves. They keep their front feet in contact with the water so that they can detect any small vibrations caused by a small fish or an insect struggling on the surface. Some raft spiders dangle their legs in the water to attract small fish.

▽ A raft spider astride a twig dangles its feet in the water to detect vibrations caused by insects that fall onto the water surface.

The story of spiders

The arachnids

Spiders belong to a group of animals called arachnids which also includes, ticks, mites and scorpions. The arachnids are related to the insects, but have a number of distinct differences. Unlike insects, arachnids do not have wings. They have four pairs of legs but no antennae, whereas insects have antennae but only three pairs of legs. There are also differences in '' ...dies and eyes of the t. ...oups.

Origin of spiders

Little is known about the origin of spiders and their ability to spin silk. It is thought that they appeared some 300 million years ago, among the first animals to live on dry land. They must have developed from animals that lived in water, but their ancestors remain a mystery.

The legend of Arachne

The ancient Greeks explained the origins of spiders by a legend. It tells of a girl called Arachne, who was changed into a spider for daring to challenge the goddess Athene to a tapestry-weaving contest and was doomed to spin for evermore.

△ Arachne is turned into a spider and doomed to spend the rest of her life spinning silk.

The ancient Greek word for a spider is "arachne," and the scientific name for the spider group, arachnids, comes from this.

Lucky spiders

Many people are afraid of spiders, even though few are dangerous to humans. In many places it is thought to be unlucky to kill a spider, and people regard them as lucky, especially the tiny money spiders.

Dancing mania

The true tarantula is a large wolf spider found around Taranto, in southern Italy. People once believed that its bite caused a disease called "tarantism." The victims were supposed to leap about and make strange noises. A superstition grew up that the best cure for this dancing mania was a lively folk dance, which became known as the tarantella.

The persistent spider

Perhaps the best known spider legend is told of Robert Bruce, a real Scottish king of the early 1300s. After many defeats by the English, he is said to have been lying in a cave when he noticed a spider attempting to swing on a thread across the entrance. Time and again it failed, but finally it succeeded. This gave Bruce heart, and he took on the English once more and defeated them in the battle of Bannockburn.

Spiders in space

In the 1970s, a number of experiments proposed by US high school students were carried out in Skylab, the orbiting space laboratory. One of these was to find out whether the lack of gravity (pulling force of earth) had any effect on the web-spinning ability of spiders. Two garden spiders, Anita and Arabella, were studied and it was found that the webs they spun in space were irregular.

△ Arabella's untidy web in space.

Facts and records

△ The female golden silk spider in her web. Just to her left, by her legs, can be seen her tiny mate.

Male and female

In general, the greatest difference between male and female spiders is their size. The female garden spider, for example, is almost twice the size of the male.

The female golden silk spider weighs about 100 times as much as her tiny mate. Strangely enough, this does not put him in danger of being eaten by the female, as happens with some kinds of spiders. He is fortunately too small to be regarded as a worthwhile meal by his mate.

Largest

The largest known spider is a bird-eating spider of tropical South America. One male specimen found had a leg span of 28 cm (11 in) and a body 9 cm (3.5 in) long. A female of the same species was found with a body length of 10 cm (4 in).

Spider population

A scientist once calculated the number of spiders in a field that had remained undisturbed for several years. He found that there were over 2 million spiders to the acre (4,047 square meters). This is equivalent to about 500 in every square meter.

A healthy appetite

Another scientific calculation has unearthed the amazing fact that the weight of insects eaten by spiders each year is more than the weight of all the people on earth.

Life span

Most spiders live only one season, a few months and usually not more than 18 months. But tarantulas can live much longer – up to 25 years! Some bird-eating spiders have been known to live for 20 years or more.

Glossary

Arachnids
The group of animals that spiders belong to.

Cocoon
The egg sac wrapped in protective silk.

Communal webs
Haphazardly made webs used by a number of spiders.

Crab spiders
Spiders, with no web, that lie in wait for their prey, camouflaged by their surrondings.

Dragline
The thread spun by a spider as it moves around. It serves as a safety line.

Egg sac
A silken bag for holding a spider's eggs.

Jumping spiders
Hunting spiders that jump on their prey.

Molt
A shedding of the skin.

Orb weavers
Spiders that spin circular, flat webs with spokes.

Palps
The two "feelers" attached to the sides of a spider's mouth. They have various uses.

Raft spider
A type of hunting spider that catches its prey on or in water.

Spiderling
A baby spider.

Spinnerets
The organs a spider uses to spin out its silk.

Stabilimenta
Bands of shiny silk some orb weavers spin across their webs.

Tarantula
At one time, the name of a certain wolf spider found in southern Italy, but now used for any of the large, hairy spiders of the tropics and subtropics.

Trap-door spiders
Spiders that hide under the ground and dart out from a trap-door to grab their prey.

Wolf spiders
Hunting spiders that chase their prey.

Index